Christian
in Poetry uñu i ulii y

Some Anglican Voices from Temple to Herbert

ROWAN WILLIAMS

SLG Press
Convent of the Incarnation Fairacres
Parker Street Oxford OX4 1TB

www.slgpress.co.uk

*Engraved glass, 'Hail the Bright Morning',
by Simon Whistler, is reproduced on the
cover by kind permission of the artist.*

ISBN-13 978-0-7283-0162-7
ISBN-10 07283-0162-8
ISSN 0307-1405

Printed by Will Print, Oxford, England.

ACKNOWLEDGEMENTS

SLG Press is grateful to the following for kind permission to print copyright material:

Carcanet Press Ltd for 'Manna', by Thomas Traherne from *The Ceremonial Law*, quoted in PN Review 124, 1998.

Faber & Faber Ltd, London, and Harcourt Brace & Company, for lines from The Dry Salvages and 'Little Gidding', by T. S. Eliot, both in *Four Quartets*, London 1944.

Mr Gwydion Thomas for poems by by R. S Thomas: 'The Bright Field' Macmillan 1972 and extracts from 'Bleak Liturgies', Bloodaxe Books, 1992.

Many of the texts quoted and referred to may be found in *Love's Redeeming Work. The Anglican Quest for Holiness*, ed. G. Rowell, K. Stevenson and R. Williams, OUP, 2001.

The following talks were first given as a seminar at the Institute of Spiritual Studies, Eastern Hill, Melbourne in 2002. Thanks are due to the Rt Revd David Farrer, Bishop of Wangaratta, for kind permission to print them as a pamphlet in the series Fairacres Publications.

I

IN THESE talks I want to introduce you to some of what I regard as the leading and formative themes in the development of Anglican identity since the sixteenth century. As you are aware that George Herbert died a couple of centuries before William Temple was thought of, you will have noticed that the title 'From Temple to Herbert' sounds a little odd. But I hope that as the theme unfolds you will see why I have chosen to approach it in this way.

There is a saying, which originates with the French Catholic poet Charles Péguy, that 'everything begins in mysticism and ends in politics'. My intention is, in a sense, to begin with politics and end with mysticism. That is to say, I would like to trace the lineaments of developing Anglican identity by beginning to look at the way in which Anglicanism has engaged with society, and from there to try and unfold how Anglicanism nurtures and preserves its sense of the divine mystery. Because to put those two figures, William Temple and George Herbert, on the table at the beginning is already to indicate one of the obvious polarities in people's perception of the Anglican tradition. On the one hand you have a figure who is manifestly a public person. Born as William Temple was into the very heart of the establishment—his father was Archbishop of Canterbury, he had been headmaster of a major public school, he had been prominent in church politics and national issues—Temple stands for a particular kind of Anglican identity which sees itself at the centre of the social order. Temple used that position to argue for reforms and re-imaginings of the social order, and it has been said with some truth that Temple has been one of the major architects of the post-war Welfare State in Britain.

But we are all aware of ways in which that tradition of engagement has not always come over quite so benignly—in

Britain or elsewhere; that the Anglican conviction of being at the centre of things doesn't do a great deal of justice to other Christians, let alone to people of other faiths or of no faith. And the assumption of effortless superiority on the part of the Church of England, both within Christendom and within British society, can be rather wearing, even for other Anglicans in the United Kingdom. But that is another story.

And then there is George Herbert, someone who turned his back very conspicuously and deliberately on public life. He had been Public Orator of Cambridge University, close to the Royal Family and the leading cultural circles of his day; yet he chose to spend the last years of his short life as a country priest, writing an unforgettable digest of advice to country clergy, and a unique corpus of poetry, the mystical intensity and contemplative imagination of which is as substantial and as striking as anything you will find in European literature.

Herbert, in one sense, turns away from the obvious social leverage that William Temple represents to a certain silence, to frustration even, and to darkness. Don't imagine for a moment (I shall return to this later) that Herbert is best represented by the sweet and quaint extracts which we sometimes sing from our hymn books. Herbert's deepest and darkest poems are very disturbing reading indeed.

So you may now see why I've chosen these two figures, in that order: Temple as standing for what is often seen as the historical essence of Anglicanism, and Herbert for another, a hidden stream, as it were, within the tradition. Do these connect? And what Christian integrity is represented by the connection? And what does that integrity have to say that is valid and important in the whole conversation of Christianity?

Now in a sense that's all I have to say, because the rest of my job will be to introduce you to a number of writers, to various passages, to themes and ideas that crop up across the centuries of Anglican history, to try and answer the question with which I have begun. And since William Temple stands first in the title, let us start by listening to him.

Here is Temple writing in the nineteen-twenties, quite early in his career, about 'Church, Christendom and Kingdom':

> The Church is the fellowship of Christ's disciples, welded together by the operation of His Spirit within them into the organised society which is His Body. It may contain a small or a large proportion of the citizens of any country where it works. Its own distinctive activity is worship, the imparting and receiving of the Word and Sacraments, and the self-dedication of its members to His service in the world. As they thus serve Him, they leaven society; and so there grows up a whole civilisation which is in greater or lesser degree Christian, in the sense that it is moulded by the principles of the Gospel. This takes place in many countries; and those countries form Christendom. The Church is not the nations, though the nations are within the Church. The difference between them is not in membership but in function. It is still the business of the Church to inspire; it is the business of the nations and their citizens to act on that inspiration in the various affairs of life.[1]

There, I suggest, is a very clear statement of that vision of Anglican identity, and indeed Christian identity, which sees the life of the church at the heart of things, pervading the structures of society, the church remaining in some sense a body given distinctness by its worship, and yet with its boundaries being fairly open. Notice Temple's statement that the difference between the nations and the church is not in membership but in function. That is a very deeply rooted Anglican idea. The church is not a society over against other societies; the church is members of one society functioning in a particular way. The roots, as I say, are very deep in Anglican history and thinking, and Temple is there giving expression to that vision which is most classically put forward just before 1600 by the great Richard Hooker for whom the church and the commonwealth were essentially one body. The church is, for Hooker, English society at prayer in England; and anywhere else the church is Scottish, or Swiss, or French, or German (or whatever national society) at prayer.

We shouldn't suppose too quickly that this means a narrow pietistic or private sense of what Christian identity and Christian worship are about. Temple was very clear about that, and in another quotation from a later work published under the title *Citizen and Churchman*, he expresses what for many people is again a classical Anglican sense of worship as the drawing together and the offering to God of what is happening in society. Temple writes there that in the Eucharist

> ... we bring familiar forms of economic wealth, which is always the product of man's labour exercised upon God's gifts, and offer them as symbols of our earthly life ...
>
> Because we have offered our 'earthly' goods to God, He gives them back to us as heavenly goods, binding us into union with Christ in that self-offering which is His royalty...
>
> The Eucharist divorced from life loses reality; life devoid of worship loses direction and power. It is the worshipping life that can transform the world.[2]

So for Temple, as for a good many other Anglican theologians of that generation around the nineteen-forties and 'fifties, the renewal of worship is itself a social and political requirement. It is to do with the offering of human goods to God so that they may be received back as divine goods, and through that receiving of divine goods, society itself is bit by bit transformed or, at the very least, soaked in some degree by the Christian vision and Christian practice.

Temple stands, as I have said, very much at the centre of the social order, consciously working from the heart of things. But it is strange to think that a vision very like Temple's can be expressed by a much more marginal character in twentieth century Anglicanism to whom I want to turn next—not at all a well-known figure for the majority of the people in the Anglican Church, even in his own country, but a theologian of remarkable originality and power. I am speaking here of the American lay theologian, William Stringfellow. A lawyer by profession, an enthusiast for art, comedy and the circus, a self-proclaimed homosexual, a man whose theological reading was extraordinarily wide, and who met the great Karl Barth when Barth visited the United States, drawing from him an endorsement for which any professional theologian would have given their right arm. (Barth, in a public discussion session in Chicago, turned to Stringfellow and said, 'This is the man America should be listening to'.)

Now Stringfellow, in his work, his witness and indeed his lifestyle a marginal person, says something rather similar to Temple in another key. And my reason for turning to Stringfellow is that he, like the great Barth, is a very consistent critic of religiousness. Like Temple, he refuses to believe that the Christian community is a community alongside others. If you take that line, Stringfellow argues, then religion becomes a human activity like other human activities. Some people like golf at the weekends and some people like religion. It is really a matter of temperament and taste and consumer choice. Stringfellow writes:

> Personally, I find no cause to be interested in mere religion. It can be a certain diversion, I admit, to speculate and argue about religious ideas and practices, but I am no longer in college, and my law practice does not often permit the luxury of hypothetical and speculative matters. It appears to me more urgent and more necessary to deal with history, that is, with actual life ... So I do not bother, as far as I am aware, with dabbling in religion. And if, as it may in my own lifetime turn out, Protestantism—like Zen or 'religious science' or other sects—is or becomes only an institution of religion devoted to its own maintenance and a practice of

5

religion for its own sake, then I am just not superstitious enough to remain a Protestant.

But when, now and then, I turn to and listen to the Bible, or when, now and then I hear the Word of God exposed in preaching, or when, now and then, I see the gospel represented in the Holy Communion ... or I discern and encounter the presence of God's Word in the ordinary affairs of everyday existence in the world—on these occasions, in these circumstances, I am reminded, if sometimes ruefully, that the gospel is no mere religion in *any* essential respect.[3]

He goes on a little later:

The Christian faith is distinguished, diametrically, from mere religion in that religion begins with the proposition that some god exists; Christianity, meanwhile, is rejoicing in God's manifest presence among us. Religion describes human beings, mind you, usually sincere and honorable and intelligent ones, searching for God or, more characteristically searching for some substitute for God—that is, some idea of what God may be like—or would be like—and then worshipping that idea and surrounding that substitution with dogma and discipline. But the gospel tells when and how and why and where God has sought us and found us and offered to take us into God's life.[4]

Strong stuff, and you can see why Karl Barth liked him. But the point that Stringfellow is making is that religion is precisely a human activity like other human activities distinguished only by its object. The focus is on what human beings do. But what if the focus is somewhere else? What if the focus is on God's action and God's initiative? Well, that may be encountered almost anywhere, and when it is encountered it is encountered in such a way as to open your eyes and sensitise your perception to see it again in other unlikely situations. And Stringfellow repeatedly contrasted being a religious person with being a biblical person. For him, being a biblical person was being someone who understood

6

that they were addressed and summoned, that they were under judgement, that God's initiative had already overtaken them, changing the whole frame of moral and spiritual reference in which they lived. And, says Stringfellow, the one thing that that is *not* about is leisure activities.

Now I hope you can see there some of the connection that there is between Temple and Stringfellow, wildly dissimilar figures in all kinds of ways, and I don't quite know how they would have got on with each other had they ever met. And yet what they had in common is precisely a resistance to the idea that faith can be compartmentalised, because that would be mere religion in Stringfellow's sense. And that means that the church has got to be something a bit more, a bit different from merely the expression of loyal, religious solidarity. And what that something more and something different might be is not easy to discern. For Temple, speaking from the heart of English establishment, it means the classic ethos of the Church of England, present, unobtrusively but very definitely and firmly, in the midst of the social order. For Stringfellow, working as a lawyer in the back streets of Harlem, living on legal aid payments for undertaking the defence of unlikely young criminals in the worst slums of New York—for Stringfellow, not surprisingly, it is a bit different from Temple. But something of the same comes across. Here is a practice of living before God which cannot simply be cordoned off into something called 'religion', with a special object called 'God' and special things which religious people do that keep God happy.

What I want to suggest is that this represents one of the earliest impulses of the Anglican Reformation. And I want to wind the reel back now to the sixteenth century, to look at some of the founding fathers of the Anglican identity in the early sixteenth century, because what I want to argue is that this unease about the church or faith or Christian religion as one area among others in human life is what pervades much

7

of the most powerful literature of the first Reformed generations in the sixteenth century.

I turn first to William Tyndale, great biblical translator and Reformed theologian, a better theologian than he is sometimes given credit for being. People know him best as a translator, as somebody who brings back into the speech of faith in English some of that salty, vernacular touch that you find in the very best of earlier, medieval writing. 'So the Lord was with Joseph, and Joseph was a lucky fellow' was one of Tyndale's great phrases from his translation of Genesis. Very often if you look at what the Authorised Version, the King James version, does with Tyndale, you will see a very consistent rear-guard action to make Tyndale's English a little bit more restrained. But Tyndale was not just a gifted, pithy and entertaining translator: he was somebody who had a profound and far-reaching vision of the social order. For Tyndale, God was shown in the world by particular kinds of social relation. The church is the community of those who live in God-like relation to one another.

The church is the community of those so overwhelmed by their indebtedness to God's free grace, that they live in a state of glad and grateful indebtedness to one another. The imagery of debt and indebtedness was one that greatly interested Tyndale, and he writes about it very eloquently in his treatise on the Parable of the Unjust Steward in Luke 17, one of the most difficult parables in the New Testament. Tyndale has a very short way with it though. For him, it is a springboard for talking about indebtedness, and he sets up this model of grateful indebtedness against what he sees as a model of Christian or religious practice and thinking which struggles to keep God in your debt. That is for him the antichrist! Any system of religious activity and thinking which tries to give you some leverage over God—'I've never denied God a moment of my time, I hope he remembers that'—such an attitude is poisonous to true faith. What is

8

more, it leads to what Tyndale regards as a kind of religious specialism. You develop and explore the whole range of specialist activities, which not everybody can perform, which become the way in which you can keep God in your debt. You create religious institutions which are designed to preserve that divine indebtedness to you, and while you are doing that, you largely ignore the concrete forms of indebtedness towards other human beings to which you ought to be attending. Now Tyndale puts this of course in blunt and practical terms. Why waste money endowing chantry chapels when you could be giving it to the poor? Why spend your life in monastic communities when your first call is to create community within the natural societies you are part of? Are not these chantries and these religious orders just an example of religious specialism trying to keep God in your debt? I hasten to add that I don't think Tyndale was entirely right, either about chantries or about religious orders. What I am trying to tease out is why he was so angry about them. And the answer to that is, I think, in terms that both William Temple and William Stringfellow might have recognised. Tyndale is protesting against 'religion', against the separation of that sphere from other spheres of human activity. Here is Tyndale, in his 'A Pathway into the Holy Scripture':

> By faith we receive of God, and by love we shed out again. And that must we do freely, after the example of Christ, without any other respect, save our neighbour's wealth [*sic* 'welfare'] only; and neither look for reward in the earth, nor yet in heaven, for the deserving and merits of our deeds as friars preach; though we know that good deeds are rewarded, both in this life and the life to come. But of pure love must we bestow ourselves, all that we have, and all that we are able to do, even on our enemies.

And Tyndale here picks up a favourite idea of Martin Luther, whose works he was reading at the time. Jesus Christ is not good and generous so that God will be nice to him. Jesus Christ is good and generous because the life of God lives in him. So then, if we live in Christ, we aren't good and generous so as to persuade God to be nice to us. We are good and generous because that's where our life lies and we can't in one sense be anything else. So to indebtedness—and I read now from another of Tyndale's *Doctrinal Treatises*, 'The Parable of the Wicked Mammon':

> The order of love or charity, which some dream, the gospel of Christ knoweth not of, that a man should begin at himself, and serve himself first, and then descend, I wot not by what steps. Love seeketh not her own profit 2 Cor. xii; but maketh a man to forget himself, and to turn his profit to another man, as Christ sought not himself, nor his own profit, but ours. This term, myself, is not in the gospel; neither yet father, mother, sister, brother, kinsman, that one should be preferred in love above another. But Christ is all in all things. Every Christian man to another is Christ himself; and thy neighbour's need hath as good right in thy goods, as has Christ himself, which is heir and lord over all. And look, what thou owest to Christ, that thou owest to thy neighbour's need. To thy neighbour owest thou thine heart, thyself, and all that thou hast and canst do. The love that springeth out of Christ excludeth no man, neither putteth difference between one and another.

And Tyndale goes on to say that your indebtedness is first to the people who are most immediately and obviously under your nose. But when he has dealt with that, he goes on: 'if thy neighbours which thou knowest be served, and thou yet have superfluity, and hearest necessity to be among your brethren a thousand miles off, to them art thou debtor'. And then, very controversially: 'yea, to the very infidels we be debtors if they need …'.

Tyndale's early Protestant editors put that in square brackets. They thought that it was just a little bit too much for anybody to take on board. But Tyndale, as you can see from the enormous energy of his style, is really getting quite carried away here. If we are really indebted to other human beings, well, we are indebted to other human beings, and there's an end of it, and if they happen to be Turks or even papists, well, never mind! We owe them what we owe Christ, and we owe Christ everything, and Christ owes God his Father everything because God bestows everything upon him as he does upon us. And so back to where we started, the obvious corollary of this is that our generosity and our goodness come from the life of Christ living in us, and are expressed in that sense of perpetual, grateful indebtedness to all. Where there is need, there is love owing.

The same theme recurs in a very different writer, about half a generation younger than Tyndale. With Edwin Sandys, who became Archbishop of York in Queen Elizabeth's reign, the idea that our social ethics is rooted in debt reappears. Indebtedness takes centre stage in Sandys's discussion of the duties of Christian people. The point in all this with Tyndale and with some of his followers is that the life of the Christian is a way of discharging social relations in such a fashion that God's love is made manifest. Tyndale's assault on late medieval monasticism, the chantry system and various other things, is really an assault on the idea that there are duties owed to God which have nothing to do with human flourishing. Remember that little phrase that he uses: 'our neighbour's wealth only'. The 'shedding of love' is to do with the welfare of the neighbour. And to interpret acts of love to mean acts of religious devotion at the expense of the practical upbuilding of community, that is, as Tyndale would see it, the work of the antichrist.

As I have said, I don't by any means endorse Tyndale's version of what monasticism amounts to. But it is possible to see, if you look at the social patterns of the late middle ages, the degree to which the monastic world, and indeed the clerical world in general, had become a fairly self-contained corporation of skilled professionals whose task was the performance of specifically religious duties. The proliferation of clergy whose job was to say mass for the departed—and nothing else—reinforces precisely that sense of the church as a kind of state within the state, another sort of nation. It has its own laws in canon law and it has its supreme magistrate in the Bishop of Rome. So Tyndale's protest against monasticism and clericalism becomes very closely interwoven with the political protest of Reformed controversialists against Catholicism seen as a kind of international political network, a para-state controlled by a foreign monarch. I don't say they were right, but that is what they saw, and that is what they objected to, partly for conventional nationalist reasons and partly for the theological reasons that Tyndale outlines.

Tyndale, however, failed to persuade Henry VIII that his theology was accurate, and though he was executed on the continent, it was with the full connivance and co-operation of Henry's government and the Bishop of London, a very sinister man called Stokesly.

You can see, then, why the three Williams, Tyndale, Temple and Stringfellow, have something in common. And it is Tyndale who gives the most vivid, the most unforgettably concrete theological anchorage for this vision in his marvellous treatise on the parable of the Unjust Steward, or as he calls it, 'The Parable of the Wicked Mammon'. When I first read that text, which was only a few years ago, it was at a time when issues of debt and indebtedness were featuring very largely in discussions of international politics and when I, like a good many others in Britain, had become very involved in the Jubilee 2000 campaign for the cancellation of international debt. And I am bound to say that Tyndale's work, which completely turns on their head assumptions which we might make about debt, is a powerful, prophetic stimulus to our thinking about the global economy. Do we think first in terms of the debt that the poor owe to the rich?

No, says Tyndale, we think first of the debt owed by the rich to the poor, because only *that* makes theological sense in the light of the God we have been led to believe in.

But now, having without any apology conscripted Tyndale for contemporary purposes, I want to turn briefly to another of the great and very listenable voices of the day, who developed some of his views a little further, and that is Hugh Latimer, Bishop of Worcester, who was martyred under Queen Mary, but in the reign of King Edward VI had been one of the most popular and influential preachers in Britain. Latimer's preaching style, like Tyndale's writing style, is colloquial and brisk and moreover often very funny indeed. Poor King Edward VI had to sit through hours and hours of sermons in his short life, but I like to think that when he saw Latimer's name on the list of the Chapels Royal his heart lifted slightly.

Latimer, like Tyndale, is a critic of the monastic philosophy that he sees around him, the closed corporation model of the religious specialist. And in one of his sermons preached at court on the Lord's Prayer he picks up a story from the Desert Fathers to illustrate how the virtues of the monastic life have to be translated into the common life of the Christian household.

> I read once the story of a holy man, (some say it was St Anthony), which had been a long season in the wilderness, neither eating nor drinking any thing but bread and water: at the length he thought himself so holy, that there should be nobody like unto him. Therefore he desired of God to know who should be his fellow in heaven. God made him answer, and commanded him to go to Alexandria; there he should find a cobbler which should be his fellow in heaven. Now he went thither and sought him out, and fell in acquaintance with him, and tarried with him three or four days to see his conversation. In the morning his wife and he prayed together; then they went to their business, he in his shop, and she about her housewifery. At dinner time they had bread and cheese, wherewith they were well content

and took it thankfully. Their children were taught to fear God and say their *Pater-noster*, and the Creed, and the Ten Commandments; and so he spent his time doing his duty truly. I warrant you, he did not so many false stitches as cobblers do now-a-days. St Anthony perceiving that, came to knowledge of himself, and laid away all pride and presumption. By this ensample you may learn that honest conversation and godly living is much regarded before God; insomuch that this poor cobbler, doing his duty diligently, was made St Anthony's fellow. So it appeareth that we be not destituted of religious houses: those which apply their business uprightly and hear God's word, they shall be St Anthony's fellows; that is to say, they shall be numbered among the children of God.

I am bound to say that Latimer treats the story from the Desert Fathers pretty freely. I don't remember the bread and cheese in the sayings of the Desert Fathers, nor indeed the cobbler, but Latimer typically makes a good, vivid and contemporary story out of it. But note that phrase, 'we be not destituted of religious houses'. He is preaching after the dissolution of the monasteries, and he is saying, 'monasteries have not been dissolved. They have gone domestic'. And the kind of manifestation of God's will and God's ways which we once looked for in monastic life, we must now look for in the life of the Christian household where people learn to say their prayers and do their duty. I think you can see how that is one particular outworking, one particular kind of reflection, on the sort of theology that Tyndale is taking for granted.

Temple, Stringfellow, Tyndale, Latimer—all of them are convinced that the graceful initiative of God in Christian life actually impacts on what the social order looks like; it impacts in such a way that you can't restrict its effects to the performance of religious duties, the doing of religious things. This confuses a doctrine of the church and a doctrine of power in many ways, and the confusion is manifest throughout Anglican history. But it is arguably quite a fruitful confusion. It means that for every Anglican writer who treats theology as a kind of ideology of the existing state of power, you are quite likely to find another writer (or even the same writer on a different page) deploying the same theology to battle against a restriction of the divine freedom or the divine initiative, which does not allow God's grace to have its proper impact on the ordinary relations of human beings in love and justice, and what Tyndale would call mutual indebtedness.

My last case study is a very different writer from somewhere in between the two chronological extremes I have already mentioned, and that is Samuel Taylor Coleridge, writing early in the nineteenth century, in an essay *On the Constitution of Church and State*. Curiously, it is a work which Coleridge's best recent biographer, Richard Holmes, totally ignores, and there are a good many readers of Coleridge as poet and critic who have failed to take up his reflections on church and state, because it is assumed that his interest in theology was something of a sideline. Anyone who has read more than a few pages of Coleridge ought to know better, but there we are.

Coleridge's essay on the constitution of church and state is a kind of crystallization of just the principles I have been trying to outline. It is a lengthy protest against the idea that there can be a single institutional, centrally-controlled Christian body called 'the church'. The church is something which exists, in one sense, in God's eyes alone; the church is a body subsisting through time, but we are very much astray when we try to identify the church that exists from God's perspective with a visible body here and now. And of course Coleridge, just like Latimer and Tyndale, is attacking a particular version of Roman Catholic theology. He doesn't mean that the church is invisible, that it is simply the sum total of everybody leading Christian lives. In every specific setting, the church has an identity of its own, because the church does distinctive things—back to William Temple and the priority of worship. The church prays, the church studies and reflects, the church offers its worship, the church intercedes. What is more, on the basis of all that, the church asks good questions, because out of this prayer and this worship the church's sense of what a human being is like gradually matures in such a way that it is equipped to ask awkward questions of the society around it. But the distinctiveness of the church lies in these activities, rather than in any clearly demarcated boundary which would say, here's the church, here's society. And in a fine phrase, Coleridge says that 'the church is the friendly opposite of society'. Wherever the church happens, wherever there is a distinctive gospel-based perspective to be offered in the social context, there is the church.

And so, while there are pragmatic ways of organizing church life in this or that setting, there are no ways of building up the church as something in itself apart from its ongoing conversation with the society around it. Here is a very vivid apologia for the Church of England as Coleridge understood it; and its theological roots, I would suggest, are very much in the vision of Tyndale and Latimer and have quite a bit to do with the vision of Temple and Stringfellow. Coleridge, who is notoriously not very easy to read, doesn't always give you wholly clear lines of argument, but if you read this essay closely enough, you will be able to tease out from it that some of these theological themes are taken for granted.

Now, as a kind of bridge into what I want to say in Part II, let me very briefly take the reflection a stage further. Thus far, I have been arguing that some of our definitive and classical Anglican writers—and I have taken examples from three different eras—are bound in common by a particular vision of the relation of church and society. It is not without its shadows and its ambiguities; that should be clear enough. Yet it has a serious theological principle at its heart, one which is quite surprisingly close to some of the ideas of Karl Barth, as William Stringfellow saw. And that principle is that the church is not about religion as a separable activity. And the commands of God, the ways in which we become not acceptable to God but aligned with God, are to do with our fundamental social relations. Replace that with a doctrine of special religious duties and you have undermined the whole point of a church which witnesses to the priority and freedom of God's action.

But in that vision of a church not bound by religiousness, there is already coming very faintly into focus a whole attitude to human experience, to the human psyche; and the bridge I want to build from this apparently political and social philosophy and vision is towards a nuanced picture of the whole human experience, which I believe comes to light in other kinds of Anglican devotion and theology. You will find it in Hooker, you will find it in Herbert, you will find it in many other poets and also in some philosophers. And it's the attitude which I would like to sum up in the phrase 'contemplative pragmatism', by which I mean an attitude of time-taking, patient, absorbing awareness of the particular situation you are in. Nothing, you may say, distinctively Anglican about that, and perhaps there isn't. But the point is, *that* is the kind of virtue that a great deal of Anglican literature, from the sixteenth century onwards, seems to inculcate: a willingness to look at apparently secular, apparently unpromising situations, to look long enough and hard enough for God to come to light. Which means, a certain suspicion of hasty, gung-ho religious language, a certain suspicion of exaggerated *religious* experience—the idea yet again that God is a really exciting leisure activity. This suspicion can turn, and in Anglican history very often did turn, into an almost deliberate cultivation of dryness and dullness. The way in which eighteenth-century Anglicans, at least, used the word 'enthusiasm' tells us a great deal;

because enthusiasm, as you will be aware, is something to be avoided at all costs by decent Anglicans. And although the word had a more robust meaning in the eighteenth century than it does today, some of the feeling has survived, as you may have noticed. And as the famous remark ascribed to Bishop Butler addressing John Wesley has it: 'Sir, the pretending to extraordinary visions and revelations of the Holy Ghost is a horrid thing, a very horrid thing!' But when one has noted all those not so edifying and not so helpful expressions, one can turn, as I shall do presently, to some less trivial and less maligned examples of that feeling: the sense that comes over very clearly in Hooker, or Herbert, or Henry Vaughan, or for that matter in T. S. Eliot and R. S. Thomas, that the work of God is something which requires an enormously selfless patience to discern, so that external experiences of failure or dryness are not necessarily the marks of spiritual failure.

Nothing particularly Anglican indeed; it is the wisdom which comes through in St John of the Cross, in Augustine Baker, the Anglo-Welsh mystic of the seventeenth century, or in Jean-Pierre de Caussade in France rather later on. But there are some very particular ways in which it emerges in the Anglican tradition, and especially I would argue, in Anglican lay theologians and writers. Another feature, to which I will return, is the degree to which Anglicanism has, from the beginning, fostered and encouraged lay theologies; sometimes theologies which are at a bit of an angle to what the hierarchy would like to see, but nonetheless vivid and interesting. And, particularly in the modern period, the inspiration which Anglicanism has given to the literary world of imagination has to be seen as part of that distinctive identity that has evolved in this Christian experiment called Anglicanism, of which we are the heirs.

II

I want now to try and cross the bridge that I have thrown out from one area to another via discourse by moving from Temple to Herbert, and to think about the way in which some of this general ethos that I have been describing affects more markedly the imaginative and spiritual lives of Anglicans from the first period onwards.

First of all a little background. The beginnings of the Anglican experiment in Britain have, as you know, very varied roots. There is not only the Continental Reformation coming in to shape the mind of Latimer and Tyndale; there are also the late medieval political movements of protest against the papacy, like the so-called Conciliarist movement, which regarded supreme authority of the church as lying with the Council of all its Bishops, not with the solitary figure of the Pope. And there is also that kind of reformist openness that was prevalent at the very beginning of the sixteenth century as people began to rediscover, for example, the vision of Plato. Those who began to read Plato around 1500 were certainly among those who helped to shape the particular course that the English Reformation would take. So it is quite a mixture of opposite extremes—the anti-culture stance of Luther, the contemplative exploration of Plato—and yet so often they are found within the same Anglican spectrum. And in speaking of the way in which the Anglican imagination in this period seeks to discern God in unexpected places, and to see the world itself as a kind of sacrament of God, you will find that, for example, in one of the great Anglican poets of the later sixteenth century, Edmund Spenser. The first piece of poetry I want to read is from Spenser's 'Hymn of Heavenly Beauty'. It is a very long poem,

but in the lines I shall read you will see how Spenser is
leading the vision up through beauty to God:

> Faire is the heaven where happy soules have place
> In full enjoyment of felicitie,
> Whence they doe still behold the glorious face
> Of the Divine Eternall Maiestie:
> More faire is that, where those Idees on hie
> Enraunged be, which Plato so admyred,
> And pure Intelligences from God inspyred.
>
> Yet fairer is that heaven, in which do raine
> The soveraigne Powres, and mightie Potentates,
> Which in their high protections doe containe
> All mortall princes and imperiall states;
> And fayrer yet, where as the royall Seates
> And heavenly Dominations are set,
> From whom all earthly governance is fet.
>
> Yet farre more faire be those bright Cherubins,
> Which all with golden wings are overdight,
> And those eternall burning Seraphins,
> Which from their faces dart out fierie light:
> Yet fairer than they both, and much more bright,
> Be th' Angels and Archangels, which attend
> On God's owne person without rest or end.
>
> These thus in faire each other farre excelling,
> As to the Highest they approach more near,
> Yet is that Highest farre beyong all telling
> Fairer than all the rest which there appeare,
> Though all their beauties ioyned together were:
> How then can mortall tongue hope to expresse
> The image of such endlesse perfectnesse?

There is Spenser at his most Platonic, the ascent of vision
through the heavenly powers, deriving not only from Plato
but, also from Pseudo-Dionysius the Areopagite, the great
imaginer of mystical theology and of the ascents of the soul

through the hierarchies of angels—Spenser at his most Platonic and, in some ways, his most early medieval. Spenser can also pick up from Plato the connections between earthly and heavenly love, and it is a surprise from one point of view to find among Spenser's sonnets—his secular love poems—the very famous sonnet on Easter, which has sometimes been used as a hymn. You have to read it remembering that this is actually a sonnet addressed to his poetic mistress. It is about love, earthly and heavenly, and in the final couplet suggests that there is a very straightforward link.

> Most glorious Lord of lyfe! That, on this day,
> Didst make thy triumph over death and sin;
> And, having harrow'd hell, didst bring away
> Captivity thence captive, us to win:
> This ioyous day, deare Lord, with ioy begin;
> And grant that we, for whom thou diddest dy,
> Being with thy deare blood clene washt from sin,
> May live for ever in felicity!
> And that thy love we weighing worthily
> May likewise love thee for the same againe
> And for thy sake, that all lyke deare didst buy,
> With love may one another entertayne!
> So let us love, deare Love, lyke as we ought:
> Love is the lesson which the Lord us taught.

It is perhaps in the middle of the seventeenth century that we find this Platonic vision of the world—the ascent through created beauty—most vividly set out in the poetry and prose of Thomas Traherne.

Traherne, who was a fairly obscure country parson, published nothing in his lifetime, and one not very interesting work appeared immediately after his death in 1674 to keep his reputation alive. But it is the poetry and prose manuscripts that have been discovered in the twentieth century which most vividly express what mattered above all to Traherne:

By this let Nurses, and those Parents that desire Holy Children learn to make them Possessors of Heaven and Earth betimes to remove silly Objects from before them, to Magnify nothing but what is Great indeed, and to talk of God to them and of His Works and Ways before they can either Speak or go. For Nothing is so Easy as to teach the Truth becaus the Nature of the Thing confirms the Doctrine. As when we say The Sun is Glorious, A Man is a Beautifull Creature, Soveraign over Beasts and Fowls and Fishes, The Stars Minister unto us, The World was made for you, etc. But to say This Hous is yours, and these Lands are another Mans and this Bauble is a Jewel and this Gugaw a fine Thing, This Rattle makes Musick etc. is deadly Barbarous and uncouth to a little Child; and makes him suspect all you say, becaus the Nature of the Thing contradicts your Words. Yet doth that Blot out all Noble and Divine Ideas ...

Centuries III, 11

A depiction of the world as something to be possessed, owned, blots out noble and divine ideas, and what we seek are words which express the nature of the thing. As when we say, 'the sun is glorious, the stars minister unto us'. Traherne again:

When I came into the Country, and saw that I had all time in my own hands, having devoted it wholy to the study of Felicitie, I knew not where to begin or End; nor what Objects to chuse, upon which most Profitably I might fix my Contemplation. I saw my self like som Traveller, that had Destined his Life to journeys, and was resolved to spend his Days in visiting Strange Places: who might wander in vain, unless his Undertakings were guided by som certain Rule; and that innumerable Millions of Objects were presented before me, unto any of which I might take my journey ... What then should I do? Even imitat a Traveller, who becaus He cannot visit all Coasts, Wildernesses, Sandy Deserts, Seas, Hills, Springs and Mountains, chuseth the most Populous and flourishing Cities, where he might see the fairest Prospects, Wonders and Rarities, and be entertained with greatest Courtesie: ...

For which caus I made it my Prayer to GOD Almighty, that He, whose Eys are open upon all Things, would guid me to the fairest and Divinest.

Centuries III, 52

Very typical of Traherne is that sense of an absolutely overflowing abundance of divine welcome and courtesy in the world around. And we see it again in his poem, 'Manna':

> And all these strange and Glorious works will be
> A Sacred Mirror of the Deitie.
> An Orient Gem the world will then be found,
> A Diadem wherwith even God is Crownd.
> The very Earth the seas the stars the skies,
> Springs, Rivers, Trees, the Brightness of our Eys
> All will be Manna to the Hungry Soul,
> Or Living Waters in a Chrystal Bowl.
> All Pleasant, all Delightfull, Angel's food
> To us, as unto God, Supremely Good
> For he beheld them when they all were New;
> And he who cannot erre, who first did view
> Their Glories, having seen them, understood.
>
> And plainly said they were exceeding Good.[5]

There's Traherne: Platonism through autobiography, reflection on childhood, and poetry, and emphasized there very particularly, not just the sense of God pouring through the ordinary perceptions of the child and of the adult, but again, that wonderful remark, 'the Nature of the Thing confirms the Doctrine': language is true when the nature of the thing confirms the doctrine. You simply point to the beauties of the world and you don't map it out as a system of things owned by some people and not by others. And I think Traherne might have had some conversation with Tyndale about that, if Tyndale's sense of indebtedness and Traherne's sense of non-possessiveness had come together.

There's just one more 'Platonic Anglican' I would like to refer to very briefly, although he is not often thought of as a great Anglican writer, or even a very staunch Anglican. In case we forget that William Shakespeare is also a Platonist of sorts, we might just recall these lines from *The Merchant of Venice:*

> ... Look how the floor of heaven
> Is thick inlaid with patines of bright gold:
> There's not the smallest orb which thou behold'st
> But in his motion like an angel sings,
> Still quiring to the young-eyed cherubins;
> Such harmony is in immortal souls;
> But whilst this muddy vesture of decay
> Doth grossly close it in, we cannot hear it.

That is the visionary side of the kind of ethos I want to think about at this stage in our reflections: that side which owes something of its inspiration to the Platonic education of the soul through beauty and through love towards the highest. But, as I hinted at the end of the last talk, there is another side to this, something which has to do with the capacity to be open to God and even to perceive God when experience on the surface doesn't seem to confirm it. The role of experience in the Reformation era is a hugely complicated historical and theological question. Luther himself has some forthright words for those who elevate experience at the expense of the cross, those who claim that the intensity of their religious emotion gives authority to their religious utterances. Luther bluntly says that if he meets such people he asks them if they are familiar with the cross of Jesus Christ, and if they know what it is like to be in hell, because, as Luther says, only if you have been in hell can you be a theologian (a statement which I think is true and should be engraved on the portals of every theological institution in the world).

So, what about the status and the nature of Christian experience? Well, a certain kind of rather debased Calvinism (certainly not Calvin's own view) suggested to some people that the assurance of God's mercy and God's grace was something which you felt. That is to say, you knew you were in God's favour because you felt you were in God's favour. And if you didn't feel you were in God's favour, you probably weren't in God's favour and were going to hell; which was very unfortunate no doubt but there was nothing you could do about it, because in Calvinism, if you are going to hell you are going to hell, and there's an end of it.

That rather bleak picture certainly infects some English Calvinists of the late sixteenth century, and the mixture of that kind of theology with a very strongly and rather uncritically biblicist approach to church order is what characterized a great deal of the Puritan wing of the English church from about 1570 to the end of the century. We are talking here about figures, some of them very substantial intellects like Thomas Cartwright of Cambridge, for whom the Bible was the model, not only of church government but of secular government, and for whom the absolute double predestination of God's will was a central axiom in theology: that is, God had already determined before the foundation of the world who was to be saved and who was to be damned. That had a number of implications, among them the rather startling conclusion, which Cartwright does not shrink from, that the law as laid down in Leviticus ought to be the law of England, including executing adulterers and so forth; and another startling conclusion, which is that it is not right to pray for all people, because there are some people it is no use praying for! If God has decided they are going to hell, then you are wasting your time if you are praying for them. Cartwright, as I say, is a formidable figure, and there is a great deal more to him than those rather hair-raising propositions might suggest. But they are there in his work, and they were part of the whole Puritan ethos. And they went (very often) with a rather wooden understanding of assurance and the need for a constant sense of being in God's favour, with the consequence that if you didn't feel you were in God's favour, you had to take that as a likely sign of God's reprobation.

Now, as you are aware, the political and ecclesial side of this is answered at length by Richard Hooker in his great treatise on ecclesiastical polity. But it is perhaps rather less well known that in some of his sermons, preached well before he started on his great work, you will already find some of his responses to these doctrines of assurance which I have just touched upon. Hooker is consistently concerned in all that he writes to defend two propositions about Christian prayer. One, that it is indeed legitimate to pray for the salvation of all, and here he is on the subject:

> There is in the knowledge both of God and man this certainty, that life and death have divided between them the whole body of mankind. What portion either of the two hath, God himself knoweth; for us he hath left no sufficient means to comprehend, and for that cause neither given any leave to search in particular who are infallibly the heirs of the kingdom of God, who castaways. Howbeit concerning the state of all men with whom we live ... we may till the world's end, *for the present*, always presume, that *as far as in us there is power to discern* what other are, and as far as any duty of ours dependeth upon the notice of their condition in respect of God, the safest axioms for charity to rest itself upon are these: 'He which believeth already is [saved];' and 'he which believeth not as yet may be the child of God.' It becometh not us 'during life altogether to condemn any man, seeing that ... there is hope of everyman's forgiveness, ... And therefore Charity which 'hopeth all things,' prayeth also for all men.[6]

So any suggestion that we should remit our prayers for all people is to be repudiated. The second theme which Hooker picks up where prayer is concerned challenges precisely this notion of assurance.

We ought to know that faith, like other aspects of our humanity, grows and changes. Faith is not something inhuman. It is bound in with our human emotions and experiences, and therefore the concrete sense of faith is not something on which we can place excessive reliance. Faith may be there but, like other aspects of our humanity, is susceptible to change and chance. We misjudge ourselves as faithless, says Hooker, when we don't see results quickly. And so we need another kind of assurance. We need the assurance that in our darkness or doubt or failure, God is faithful. And here he is, in two passages from a sermon preached in the fifteen-seventies.

A grieved spirit therefore is no argument of a faithless mind. ... [An] occasion of men's misjudging themselves, as if they were faithless when they are not, is, they fasten their cogitation on the distrustful suggestions of the flesh, whereof finding great abundance in themselves, they gather thereby, Surely unbelief hath full dominion, it hath taken possession of me; if I were faithful it could not be thus: not marking the motions of the Spirit and of faith, because they lie buried and overwhelmed with the contrary: when notwithstanding as the blessed Apostle doth acknowledge (Rom. viii. 26, 27), that 'the Spirit groaneth,' and that God heareth when we do not; so there is no doubt, but that our faith may have and hath her privy operations secret to us, in whom, yet known to him by whom they are.

Tell this to a man that hath a mind deceived by too hard an opinion of himself, and it doth but augment his grief: he hath his answer ready, Will you make me think otherwise than I find, than I feel in myself? I have thoroughly considered and exquisitely sifted all the corners of my heart, and I see what there is; never seek to persuade me against my knowledge; 'I do not, I know I do not believe'.

Well, to favour them a little in their weakness; let that be granted which they do imagine; be it that they are faithless and without belief. But are they not grieved for their unbelief? They are. Do they not wish it might, and also strive that it may, be otherwise? We know they do. Whence

cometh this, but from a secret love and liking which they
have of those things that are believed?[7]

In other words, if you are worried about your unbelief, you
don't disbelieve. If you want to believe, you believe. If your
will and your longing still turns towards the objects of belief,
well, belief is what you have, secretly, in a complex and
hidden way, but truly and really. He goes on,

The faith therefore of true believers, though it have many
and grievous downfalls, yet doth it still continue invincible;

And later on in the same sermon:

Yet if we could reckon up as many evident, clear,
undoubted signs of God's reconciled love towards us as
there are years, yea days, yea hours, past over our heads; all
these set together have not such force to confirm our faith,
as the loss, and sometimes the only fear of losing a little
transitory goods, credit, honour, or favour of men,—a small
calamity, a matter of nothing,—to breed a conceit, and such
a conceit as it not easily again removed, that we are clean
crost out of God's book, that he regards us not, that he
looketh upon others, but passeth by us like a stranger to
whom we are not known. Then we think, looking upon
others, and comparing them with ourselves, Their tables are
furnished day by day; earth and ashes are our bread: they
sing to the lute, and they see their children dance before
them; our hearts are heavy in our bodies as lead, our sighs
beat as thick as a swift pulse, our tears do wash the beds
wherein we lie: the sun shineth fair upon their foreheads;
we are hanged up like bottles in the smoke, cast into
corners like the sherds of a broken pot: tell not us of the
promises of God's favour, tell such as do reap the fruit of
them; they belong not to us, they are made to others. The
Lord be merciful to our weakness, but thus it is.
    Well, let the frailty of our nature, the subtilty of Satan,
the force of our deceivable imaginations be, as we cannot
deny that they are, things that threaten every moment the
utter subversion of our faith; faith notwithstanding is not
hazarded by these things.[8]

The text books tell you that just occasionally Hooker's written style is rather turgid. I think that the vividness of language in these sermons should be a corrective to any such opinion. That wonderful evocation of depression, comparing oneself with others: 'Their tables are furnished day by day; earth and ashes are our bread', is surely one of Hooker's finest prose moments. But the point that Hooker is making in all this is that precisely because Christian faith urges us and enables us to take the most comprehensive view possible of what we are, we can't lift up a moment of depression or loss or failure and say, 'That tells me once and for all who or what I am, that determines my eternal fate'. Hooker urges us, in this sermon and elsewhere in his writing, to turn to the deepest longings, the deepest motivations of our hearts. What do we really want? Are we content with unbelief, because if we are *not* content, we are not unbelievers.

Hooker, then, is going beyond the Puritan position, not just at the level of church politics, but at the level of individual, pastoral psychology. And it is important to remember that all of his work, including the many hundreds of thousands of words in *The Lawes of Ecclesiasticall Politie*, is motivated in this way. Those two principles about prayer remain central: that prayer can and must be offered for all, because the grace of God is not limited and certainly not limited in our present apprehension of it; and that our feelings moment by moment do not determine our ultimate standing before God. We have to dig deeper to find what it is we most lastingly want and long for.

And so I turn at last with much joy to Herbert, because it is at this point, I think, that George Herbert's theology and spirituality come into their own. I said in the first talk that we sometimes judge Herbert too readily by the verses we turn into hymns, which tend to be the more positive, the less wrenching of his works. But if you read the whole of Herbert's poetic composition, you will see very clearly how his abandonment of a successful career continued to simmer in his mind and his heart and cause great pain; how his sense of a brick wall in his prayer life and his pastoral life threw him back again and again on the question of whether he had made the right decision; how so much of his own piety is, in fact, shadowed by that pervasive sense of loss. And the two sides of Herbert's work are inseparable. The George Herbert who so clearly says, 'Teach me my God and King in all things thee to see'; the George Herbert who, like Spenser, has a deep and profound conviction that the beauty and order of things leads you Godwards; this is the same George Herbert who writes the five great 'Affliction' poems, the poem 'Perseverance' unpublished in his lifetime, the great expostulation of 'The Collar': 'I struck the board, and cried, no more', and many other poems of protest, loss and doubt which so shadow all his work. Here is one of the 'Affliction' poems :

> My heart did heave, and there came forth, *O God!*
> By that I knew that thou wast in the grief,
> To guide and govern it to my relief,
>> Making a scepter of the rod:
>>> Hadst thou not had thy part,
> Sure the unruly sigh had broke my heart.

> But since thy breath gave me both life and shape,
> Thou knowst my tallies; and when there's assign'd
> So much breath to a sigh, what's then behinde?
>> Or if some yeares with it escape,
>>> The sigh then onely is
> A gale to bring me sooner to my blisse.

> Thy life on earth was grief, and thou art still
> Constant unto it, making it to be
> A point of honour, now to grieve in me,
>> And in thy members suffer ill.
>>> They who lament one crosse,
> Thou dying dayly, praise thee to thy losse.

A very tightly compressed poem: to cry 'O God', not prayerfully but in despair, shows that God is in the despair. God on earth lives in grief, but because the body of Christ participates in the life of Christ, then the grief and suffering of all Christ's members belong to him. And if you lament only the cross of Calvary, you forget that Christ dies daily in the suffering and loss of all people. And you praise God inadequately if you concentrate your prayers only on the cross of Calvary as one distant event.

> They who lament one crosse,
> Thou dying daily, praise thee to thy losse.

That, of course, is Herbert a little bit at arm's length from the immediate experience of affliction. There are other poems which could be read here but which, I have to say, I find quite difficult to read in public. You have to forgive me that, but I turn to the poem, unpublished in his lifetime, 'Perseverance', because it ends with a very deeply personal moment. Perseverance, of course, is precisely what Hooker is recommending, what Herbert understands; perseverance in the sense of continuing by faithful act of the will to believe that God is gracious, and to hold to that belief whatever ups and downs may be characteristic of the inner life.

> My God, the poore expressions of my Love
> Which warm these lines & serve them vp to thee
> Are so, as for the present I did moue,
>   Or rather as thou mouedst me.

> But what shall issue, whither these my words
> Shal help another, but my iudgment bee,
> As a burst fouling-peece doth saue the birds
>   But kill the man, is seald with thee.

> ffor who can tell, though thou hast dyde to winn
> And wedd my soule in glorious paradise,
> Whither my many crymes and vse of sinn
>   May yet forbid the banes and bliss?

Onely my soule hangs on thy promisses
With face and hands clinging vnto thy brest,
Clinging and crying, crying without cease,
    Thou are my rock, thou art my rest.

A very violent image in the second stanza there—the words
are, Herbert believes, moved by God in some instances—this
is a pious poem, this is a religious poem, reader, but is it? Is it
going to help anybody, or is it more like a gun exploding
during a hunt? The birds fly away safely; but the hunter is
killed. Is that what the poet is doing—discharging something
which expresses the ruin of his own soul? Who can tell? But,
'onely my soule hangs on thy promisses'.

There is an infamous essay by the late Monsignor Ronald
Knox in which he suggests that Herbert was an easy poet of
sweet and melodious rhymes, inferior to Richard Crashaw. If
you know anything about seventeenth-century literature, I
hope you are as outraged as I am. Well, you will see perhaps
why I connect Herbert with Hooker, with these arguments
about assurance and feeling. You will see that these represent
the 'shadow side' of the Platonic commitment to seeing God
in the immediate environment; because the challenge to the
wonderful paradisal Platonism of Spenser or of Traherne is
this: if God is in the environment, what if the environment
looks terrible? What is going on? How can I believe that God
is faithfully present in the glory and beauty of creation,
pouring out, as Traherne says, 'angels food upon us' when I
have no sense of his presence? Well, the answer is, 'With face
and hands clinging unto thy breast. Clinging and crying,
crying without cease'. And digging down again and again for
those deepest sources of longing and desire and obstinate
blind faithfulness.

So the poetry of Herbert is linked at a very deep level, I
would say, to the theology of Hooker in that respect. I think
there is some difference of nuance between them, but both in
different ways, provide an answer to what I have called a

32

kind of debased Calvinism. I want to suggest that that particular kind of nuance is one of the things which helps the Anglican identity to survive one of the biggest challenges in the seventeenth century to its integrity and its very existence, namely that of the Commonwealth period when the Episcopal Church of England was proscribed and persecuted; and when those who had perhaps too readily lived in a 'William Temple' style of world suddenly found that they were no longer at the centre of things, they were no longer deciding the fate of the country. And the last poet from the seventeenth century whom I want to mention here is someone whose main work comes from a slightly later period than Herbert, but who in style stands very close to him. I am talking here of Henry Vaughan.

I am very happy to speak of Vaughan as a local boy made good! He describes himself as a 'Silurist', that is somebody from Siluria in South-east Wales. He was a physician in general practice, not very far from Brecon, and every time I visit Brecon Cathedral, I go past the grave of Henry Vaughan just off the main Abergavenny road, and make a small obeisance of the spirit as I go past. Vaughan lived through the Commonwealth, lived to see the church deprived of its privileges and its powers, and in his poetry he expresses again both the inner and the outer sense of loss that goes with this. Here he is writing, during the Commonwealth period, a poem of amazing boldness in its spiritual imagery, because he reaches straight for the imagery of the Song of Songs to describe the state of the church as the state of the abandoned mistress in the Song of Songs; and the restoration of the church can only come when the bridegroom once again returns to the church.

> Ah! he is fled!
> And while these their *mists* and *shadows* hatch,
>   My glorious Head
> Doth on those hills of Myrrhe and Incense watch.

Haste, haste, my dear!
The Souldiers here
Cast in their lots againe.
That seamlesse coat,
The Jewes touch'd not,
These dare divide and stain.

O get thee wings!
Or if as yet, until these clouds depart,
And the day springs,
Thou think'st it good to tarry where thou art,
Write in thy bookes,
My ravish'd looks,
Slain flock, and pillag'd fleeces;
And haste thee so,
As a young Roe
Upon the mounts of spices.

That is a lament for 'The British Church' and a plea that
Christ will turn his merciful eyes upon it. But Vaughan goes
far deeper than that, in his long poem, 'The Nighte' in which
he again uses imagery from the Song of Songs, to describe the
soul's longing for God

... Dear night! this world's defeat;
The stop to busie fools; cares check and curb;
The day of spirits; my soul's calm retreat
    Which none disturb!
    Christ's progess, and his prayer time;
    The hours to which high Heaven doth chime.

God's silent, searching flight
When my Lord's head is filled with dew, and all
His locks are wet with the clear drops of night;
    His still, soft call;
    His knocking time; the soul's dumb watch,
    When spirits their fair kindred catch.
    Were all my loud, evil days
Calm and unhaunted as is thy dark tent,
Whose peace but by some *Angel's* wing or voice

34

Is seldom rent;
Then I in Heaven all the long year
Would keep, and never wander here.

But living where the sun
Doth all things wake, and where all mix and tyre
Themselves and others, I consent and run
To ev'ry myre;
And by this world's ill guiding light,
Erre more than I can do by night.

There is in God, some say,
A deep but dazzling darkness; as men here
Say it is late and dusky, because they
See not all clear.
O for that night! where I in him
Might live invisible and dim!

What I am suggesting in reading these poems is that the pervasiveness of the sense of God, the refusal to tie God down to the positive moments, the religious moments, the meaningful moments, is bound up with that wider vision which I sketched earlier of the life of the church as something other than just a portion of human life. Here is the personal correlative of the political, the transition from Temple to Herbert. And as I also suggested earlier, there is something here particularly apt or appropriate to a lay spirituality. Vaughan, as I have said, was a physician not a priest; and it is often lay writers, of poetry and prose, who are able to give some kind of expression to this end of the Anglican vision: to that 'contemplative pragmatism' I mentioned earlier, to that sense that in all things God waits, and if we wait, then somehow the two waitings become attuned.

To turn now to the twentieth century, T.S. Eliot was often regarded as an extremely ecclesiastical sort of layman. He was after all, a churchwarden, but let us treat him as a layman for these purposes, and from many possible passages I give you just two from the 'Four Quartets'.

Men's curiosity searches past and future
And clings to that dimension. But to apprehend
The point of intersection of the timeless
With time, is an occupation for the saint—
No occupation either, but something given
And taken, in a lifetime's death in love,
Ardour and selflessness and self-surrender.
For most of us, there is only the unattended
Moment, the moment in and out of time,
The distraction fit, lost in a shaft of sunlight,
The wild thyme unseen, or the winter lightning
Or the waterfall, or the music heard so deeply
That it is not heard at all, but you are the music
While the music lasts. These are only hints and guesses,
Hints followed by guesses; and the rest
Is prayer, observance, discipline, thought and action.
The hint half guessed, the gift half understood, is Incarnation.

('The Dry Salvages', V)[9]

With the drawing of this Love and the voice of this Calling

We shall not cease from exploration
And the end of all our exploring
Will be to arrive where we started
And know the place for the first time.
Through the unknown, remembered gate
When the last of earth left to discover
Is that which was the beginning;
At the source of the longest river
The voice of the hidden waterfall
And the children in the apple-tree
Not known, because not looked for
But heard, half heard in the stillness
Between two waves of the sea.
Quick now, here now, always—

('Little Gidding', IV)[10]

The 'condition of complete simplicity' which Eliot goes on
to evoke after those words, and that little phrase that he picks

up from earlier on in the *Quartets*, 'Quick now, here now, always'—this captures surely one of the most unforgettable characteristics of the poetry of the twentieth century, of this vision of a God who will not be restricted but whose presence is so elusive, so dark and so mysterious precisely because it is everywhere, and not obvious, because it is not to be restricted to a religious area, to that safe territory which is marked off as just God's.

Eliot is a layman, like Vaughan, but of course priests do also write poems, even in the twentieth century, and perhaps in the twenty-first too, and you won't be entirely surprised if I turn to R.S. Thomas at this point for a little more illumination of darkness.

R.S. Thomas, who died in 2000, was probably the most significant Welsh poet writing in English, and one of the most significant presences in English poetry altogether in the twentieth century. He continued to write with extraordinary power and vividness right up to within a few months of his death. And in those last years, and months, the writing becomes a little gentler than that which is sometimes associated with him. He is famously an austere writer, and loved to adopt the persona of an old curmudgeon. I think this was a fairly deliberate act on his part, and enough memories remain with those who knew him of another kind of personality; but he quite enjoyed playing the part of someone moving almost entirely in emotional and intellectual dark and dryness:

> Why no! I never thought other than
> That God is that great absence
> In our lives, the empty silence
> Within, the place where we go
> Seeking, not in hope to
> Arrive or find. He keeps the interstices
> In our knowledge, the darkness
> Between stars. His are the echoes
> We follow, the footprints he has just

Left. We put our hands in
His side hoping to find
It warm. We look at people
And places as though he had looked
At them, too; but miss the reflection.[11]

There is an entire theology, not to say metaphysics, in those last three lines. And sometimes in R.S.'s poetry there is an unexpected echo of the Platonic vision, of beauty breaking through and leading on, and so as not to confine him too much to the darker moments, here is a poem called 'The Bright Field':

I have seen the sun break through
to illuminate a small field
for a while, and gone my way
and forgotten it. But that was the pearl
of great price, the one field that had
the treasure in it. I realise now
that I must give all that I have
to possess it. Life is not hurrying
on to a receding future, nor hankering after
an imagined past. It is the turning
aside like Moses to the miracle
of the lit bush, to a brightness
that seemed as transitory as your youth
once, but is the eternity that awaits you.[12]

R.S. was somebody who never settled very comfortably in the church at any period of his life, and many of his parishioners in a series of country parishes in north and west Wales would have said that he was one of the least comfortable parish priests you could ever imagine. But his discomfort was as much with modernisers as with traditionalists. And in late life he had some very hard things to say about the mere modernising of the language of faith; in 'Bleak Liturgies' (1992) there are references to the church in Wales which make me wince:

Do we seek to plug the hole
in faith with faith's substitute

grammar? And are we to be saved

by translation? As one by one
the witnesses died off
they commended their metaphors

to our notice. For two thousand
years the simplistic recipients
of the message pointed towards

the reductionist solution. We devise
an idiom more compatible with
the furniture departments of our churches.

> Instead of the altar
> The pulpit. Instead
> of the bread the fraction
> of the language. And God
> a shadow of himself
> on a blank wall. Their prayers
> are passing of hands
> over their brows as though
> in an effort to wipe sin
> off. Their buildings
> are in praise of concrete
> and macadam. Frowning
> upon divorce, they divorce
> art and religion.
> Ah, if one flower
> had been allowed to grow
> between the wall
> and the railings, as a sacrament
> of renewal. Instead
> two cypresses ail
> there, emaciated as the bodies
> of the thieves upon Calvary
> but with no Saviour between them.

The gaps in belief are filled
with ceremonies and processions.

The organ's whirlwind follows
Upon the still small voice

Of conviction, and he is not
in it. Our marriage
was contracted in front
of a green altar in technology's

childhood, and light entered
through the plain glass of
the wood's window as quietly
as a shepherd moving among his flock.

Faith can remove mountains,
So can cordite. But faith
heals. So does valium's
loosening of the taut nerves ....

And when the computers that are our spies
have opened to us from the inside
he is not there; the walls fall apart

and there are only the distances
stretching away. We have captured position
after position, and his white flag

is a star receding from us
at light's speed. Is there another way
of engaging? There are those who,

thinking of him in the small hours
as eavesdropping their hearts
and challenging them to come forth,

have found, as the day dawned,
his body hanging upon the crossed tree
of man, as though he were a man, too.[13]

R.S. at his most savage and yet at the end there, a profoundly
characteristic set of metaphors—the receding of God at the
speed of light; and yet somehow if you sit out the night, there

is something to be seen in the morning. And the morning hasn't come yet—that's what sitting out the night means. Occasionally during the night, as with the bright field, you have a faint glimpse of what morning might look like, and that's about as far as it goes.

A bleak translation, you might think, of the vision I have been outlining; yet there is some flow of continuity in it. R.S. Thomas and William Temple again appear to be at opposite extremes, so it appears, but what they are both battling against is the confinement of God. In their different ways they are both witnessing to this priority of divine freedom and divine initiative, God's capacity to be anywhere and everywhere. And if that is so, it is also God's freedom to show who and what God is, not in religious places but in the stuff of human relation, and in the stuff of the material world. Platonism helps you to understand this up to a point, but it is not enough. You need, as well as Platonism, what has sometimes been thought to be its opposite, a theology of the cross, a theology of God's grief, as in Herbert's poem 'Affliction'. And so Christian theology, this poetic voice seems to say, is always a theology from the cross. The theological voice, the poetic voice, speaks out that divine self-giving. Thus it is just another form of that Christian action which, for Tyndale, witnesses to God's self-bestowal on creation.

And to return to the question, is there anything specifically Anglican about this? Well, if you mean do you have to be an Anglican to understand theology and poetry in this way, of course you don't. But if we ask whether there is something which gives a particular flavour to some of the most deeply characteristic literature of the Anglican tradition, I think the answer is, yes. And to try and see how this Anglican voice weaves its way between the poetic and the political can be, at a time when both poetic and political language are often debased, one of the most substantial gifts

41

that our tradition has to offer to that wider Christian conversation which I mentioned earlier.

There are many more witnesses I have not called upon here. My goal has been, first and foremost, to offer some sense of an Anglican vision, not perhaps wholly coherent but continuously emerging across the centuries, articulated not just by prelates or by professional theologians, but by the voices of Christian imagination which still echo in our hearts and minds today.

NOTES

[1] William Temple, *Personal Religion and the Life of Fellowship,* Longman's, Green & Co., London, 1926, pp. 2-3.

[2] William Temple, *Citizen and Churchman,* London, 1941, pp. 100-3.

[3] *A Keeper of the Word: Selected Writings of William Stringfellow* (ed. Bill Wylie Kellermann), Grand Rapids, Michigan, USA, 1994, pp. 119-22.

[4] Ibid.

[5] Thomas Traherne, *The Ceremonial Law,* PN Review 124,1998, pp. 27-28.

[6] Richard Hooker, *Of the Laws of Ecclesisatical Politie,* V. xlix. 2-3.

[7] Sermon I, 'Of the Certainty and Perpetuity of Faith in the Elect' ibid. vol. III pp. 474-6.

[8] Ibid .pp.479-81.

[9] T. S. Eliot, *Four Quartets,* Faber & Faber Ltd., London, 1944.

[10] Ibid.

[11] Ronald Stuart Thomas, 'Via Negative', in *H'm,* Macmillan, London, 1972, p. 16.

[12] Ronald Stuart Thomas, *Laboratories of the Spirit,* Macmillan, London, 1972, p. 60.

[13] Ronald Stuart Thomas, *Mass for Hard Times,* Bloodaxe Books, Newcastle-upon-Tyne, 1992.